Original title:
The Purpose of Life Is to Ask Questions

Copyright © 2025 Creative Arts Management OÜ
All rights reserved.

Author: Beckett Sinclair
ISBN HARDBACK: 978-1-80566-072-9
ISBN PAPERBACK: 978-1-80566-367-6

The Art of Wondering

Why is there a sky that's blue?

And why can cows moo but not stew?

What makes the toast so brown and crisp?

Is it the sun or just a whisk?

Each Step a Query

Why do shoes have laces at all?

Can fish really swim without a call?

When birds chirp, what secrets do they share?

Is it gossip or just some fresh air?

The Unfolding Quest

Why do we park on driveways, it's odd?

Yet in the yard, we plant a pod?

What makes a cat sit upright wise?

Are they plotting? Or just chasing flies?

Journey of a Thousand Thoughts

Is chocolate a food or a dream come true?

Can spoons be jealous of forks in the stew?

When clocks tick, what do they really say?

Do they just want to tick-tock all day?

Turning Stones of Belief

I turned a stone, found a flea,
It looked at me, said, "Who's he?"
I asked the rock, it just sat still,
Life's quirks unfold, with time to kill.

I poked a twig, it snapped in glee,
"Is there a stone that sings, oh me?"
I laughed aloud, a squirrel frowned,
The world's a riddle, spinning 'round.

The Map of the Unasked

I drew a map with lots of lines,
Each path leads where confusion shines.
At crossroads marked with silly signs,
"Ask a question? Simply dine!"

A dotted route toward silly quests,
Found laughter's treasure, and much jest.
I asked a cloud about the rain,
It laughed and poured on silly pain.

Unveiling Hidden Mysteries

I peeked behind the curtain's sway,
Found socks that danced and ran away.
"What's their secret?" I did inquire,
They whispered back, "We just expire!"

A cat in boots joined in the fun,
Asked why the baked beans weigh a ton.
With every question slipped in jest,
The answers laughed, we all were blessed.

Threads of Inquiry

In webs of thought, I found a thread,
It led to where the answers fled.
I tugged a bit, it snapped in glee,
"Why questions grow like weeds?" said "We."

The more I pulled, the more it spun,
A tapestry of laughs begun.
"What is the best pie to bake?" I asked,
The answer? Smiles — too sweet to bask!

Curiosity's Compass

Why is the sky blue and not green?
Is it because someone forgot to clean?
If trees could talk, what tales would they spin?
Do squirrels laugh when they see us grin?

Are there lost socks taking a vacation?
Do they dance in drawers, full of elation?
What if my cat is secretly wise?
Plotting world domination, oh what a surprise!

Navigating the Unknown

How deep is the ocean? A question so grand,
Can mermaids help with the driftwood on land?
Why do they call it a 'fast food' meal?
When the only thing fast is how we feel?

If I eat a whole pizza, will I grow taller?
Can I blame the crust if my jeans get smaller?
Where do the sunsets go at the end of the day?
Do they get tired, sleepy, and fade away?

The Language of Questions

Why do we yawn when we're not even tired?
Is it our body's way of feeling inspired?
Do dogs dream of chasing all the tall cats?
Or do they plot schemes with their friendly rats?

What if goldfish ponder life's little tricks?
Swimming in circles, making all sorts of flicks?
Where do our thoughts go when we have to sneeze?
Do they fly out like birds, taking a tease?

Between Certainty and Wonder

Is grass really greener on the other side?
Or just an illusion in which we confide?
If clouds are made of cotton, can we jump up high?
Land in a field of fluff, oh my oh my!

What if the moon is just cheese on a plate?
Waiting for astronauts to come dine and create?
Do fish in tanks know they're part of a show?
Watching the humans come and go, oh so slow!

Breaching the Walls of Assumption

Why is the sky so blue today?
Is it the ocean's wild display?
Or did a painter lose his brush?
And left us all in quite a hush?

What if cats rule the world, you see?
They'd have a throne made of soft fleece, maybe!
And dogs would be their loyal knights,
Barking for treats, oh what delights!

Is it weird that I ask my toast
If it wants to dance with a ghost?
It never answers, it just burns,
But still I ask, for wisdom yearns!

If broccoli feels all alone,
Can we call it the vegetable throne?
I'll serve it up with a side of fries,
And ponder still, through the greasy lies.

The Light that Curiosity Casts

Why does the moon prefer the night?
Maybe it's shy of the sun's bright light?
Or is it just playing a cool game,
Hiding away while the stars get fame?

Do fish in the ocean ever dream,
Of flying high with a mighty scream?
Or swimming in clouds, feeling so free,
"It's quite a splash!" I would agree!

Can ants ever get tired of marching?
Or is there gossip they're always arching?
I'd ask them for tea, but they're too small,
And they might just eat the whole thing, after all!

If waffles and pancakes had a fight,
Which one would bring syrup for a bite?
Together they'd rule the breakfast scene,
In a food court kingdom, fit for a queen!

Seekers on a Journey

Why does the sun rise every day?
Does it have a mortgage to pay?
Or is it just running a grand race,
To beat the night with a sun-kissed face?

Can squirrels share their lofty view?
From branches high, what do they do?
Do they see dreams in acorn piles,
Or plan their escape with cheeky smiles?

Do clouds ever quibble on their way,
Debating where they'll settle and stay?
"Let's block the sun for just a while!"
"Oh no! That would ruin my style!"

Is it wise for penguins to slide?
When every crack could be their ride?
Yet still they leap with joy so bright,
In a frosty land, what a silly sight!

Whispers in the Dark

What do shadows whisper at night?
Secrets of mischief and pure delight?
Or do they recount the day's silly deeds,
Of tripping and laughing at our fast speeds?

What if the pillows talk when we sleep?
They'd gossip about dreams, secrets to keep.
"Did you see the wild cat at dusk?"
"Oh yes! He danced in glitter and musk!"

Do socks ever plot when they go missing?
Planning adventures, never dismissing?
"Let's sneak away to a land of fluff!"
Where the laundry's light, and never too tough!

If clocks could giggle and tickle our minds,
They'd tell us it's just a matter of times.
"Don't rush," they'd say with a tick and a tock,
"There's always more riddles to unlock!"

The Melody of Wonder

Why does toast always land down?
Is it the crumbs that make it frown?
Do socks go missing on a quest?
Or do they hide because they're stressed?

Why do ducks always waddle so?
Is it the weight of their own ego?
Do cows have secret dance routines?
Or is that just how the grass leans?

Can cats really see in the dark?
Is that why they play with a spark?
Could it be they don't want to sleep?
Or are they plotting just to creep?

Why do we laugh at silly things?
Like dancing bears or rubber wings?
Is it the joy that makes us grin?
Or the wild world that we begin?

Sailing on Questions

Looking for answers in the tide,
Have fish ever had a silly ride?
Do whales giggle when they dive deep?
Or do they just silently creep?

What do clouds do when it rains?
Do they dance a jig or play games?
Why does the wind like to tease us?
Is it because it knows more than us?

Can trees really talk to each other?
Do they share tales like a friendly mother?
Why do birds chirp such odd tunes?
Are they planning to take over the moons?

If life's a puzzle, what's our piece?
Is it laughter, or just silent peace?
In a game of tag, do we ever win?
Or is life just where the fun begins?

A Universe in Every Question

Do fish ever ponder their own fate?
Or are they too busy to contemplate?
Can ants really lift things so grand?
Or do they just flex on the sand?

Is time just a big old rubber band?
Stretch it far, or let it stand?
What if laughter holds the key?
Unlocking secrets, wild and free?

Why do people talk to their pets?
Are we really just their silly sets?
Can we ask the moon for a dance?
Or will it just leave us to chance?

If unicorns lived, what would they do?
Would they play hide and seek with you?
Can questions lead us to the stars?
Or do they just drive us near to bars?

Riddles in the Silence

Why do we whisper in the night?
Is it because we're scared of the light?
Do shadows hold secrets we fear?
Or are they just waiting near?

Why does silence make us so wise?
Can it be a friend in disguise?
What do crickets think of our fuss?
Do they laugh or just make a fuss?

Why do we stumble on our words?
Do thoughts fly like free little birds?
Can we ever solve the great mystery?
Or are we just part of the history?

If questions are riddles in the mist,
Do we ever find answers that exist?
In the end, do we laugh or cry?
Or just scratch our heads and wonder why?

Wisdom in Wondering

Why did the chicken cross the street?
To ponder why it's not in a seat!
Questions swirl in the breeze,
With giggles dancing like silly bees.

Do fish ever have a mid-life dread?
Asking if the sea is really their bed?
Curiosity tickles the brain,
In this wild, whimsical domain.

Is a hotdog a sandwich, you ask?
This ponderous thought is quite the task!
Skip the answers, let's just play,
And ride this crazy questioning wave!

In the quest for truth, we play like kids,
With silly grins and laughter amid.
So bring your queries and wear a hat,
For wisdom blossoms where questions are at!

Questions Carrying Stars

If stars could sing, what's their tune?
Would they hum tunes to the light of the moon?
Or ask the skies why they're so bright,
Giggle at comets in their flight?

Why does a cat knock things off shelves?
To explore the depth of its feline self?
With mischievous eyes and a curious swish,
What secrets do they hide in each little wish?

Can clouds be held in a jar, just so?
To save them for rainy days? Who knows!
Questions like kites, fly high and far,
Chasing dreams, we're wishing on stars.

What's the meaning of socks gone astray?
Asking if laundry has its own play?
With a laugh, we consider each twist,
For answers may linger in questions unmissed.

The Tapestry of Wonder

What thread am I in this grand design?
Stitched together with laughter and wine?
Each knot a question, each color a wish,
In this tapestry, nothing's amiss!

Can a rainbow make up its mind?
To be a light or a prancing find?
Sprinkling joy as it arches high,
With a wink at the clouds passing by.

If pickles loved dancing, what would they do?
Would they twirl in a jar, just for you?
Silly thoughts weave through the air,
As we stitch together what's quirky and rare.

With every wonder, a story we pick,
Through giggles and laughs, we figure the trick.
The beauty's in questions, so witty and bright,
Crafting a tapestry of pure delight!

Layers of Mystique

How many licks does it take to a see?
If we can discover the sweet mystery.
The universe chuckles, it's all in good fun,
In a game where the questions just never are done.

Why do ducks waddle, not walk straight?
Are they lost in their own feathery fate?
With a splash of humor, they quack out loud,
Spreading giggles, a merry little crowd.

Is a potato a vegetable, or an imposter?
Asking if it dreams of being a lobster!
Layered with doubt, hilarity grows,
While pondering thoughts that tickle our toes.

In the garden of queries, we laugh and we play,
Each layer unfolding like a sunbeam's ray.
So grab some questions, don't be shy,
In this maze of fun, together we'll fly!

When Wonder Meets Mystery

Why do socks vanish in the wash?
Is there a portal for the lost?
Does that pizza hold the key to truth?
Or is it just the cheese that's glossed?

Where do all the good pens go?
They vanish into thin air!
Are they building a secret lair?
Should I join them, in my spare?

Why does the toast always land face down?
Is it playing a trick on me?
Do crumbs dance in a hidden town?
And what's with that last cup of tea?

Could fish really have tales to tell?
Do they giggle in their fishy way?
Or do they simply keep it swell?
Checking their scales for the next play!

The Pulse of Curiosity

What makes the world spin so fast?
Is gravity having a laugh?
Do clouds get together for a blast?
Or do they just take a warm bath?

Why do cats knock things off the shelf?
Is it a game or some lost art?
Are they plotting to free themselves?
Or just showing they have a heart?

Do squirrels hold parliament in trees?
And where's all that energy from?
Do they drink coffee or munch on cheese?
Or do they run on pure fun?

Why's the sky blue and not plaid?
Did someone forget to mix the dyes?
Will we ever know what's truly rad?
Or just keep asking, and eat our fries?

The Poetry of Inquiry

Is that a door, or just a wall?
What if it opens to nowhere?
Shall I knock, or just recall?
Maybe I'll find a friend there!

Why are we told to clean our plates?
What if they're just working hard?
Do they gossip about their fates?
Or are they secretly a bard?

Do plants really soak up all our chat?
Is that why they never complain?
Do they giggle or just sit flat?
And what's the deal with the rain?

What if the moon has a grumpy face?
Is it tired of our stare?
Does it dream of other places?
Or just wonder if we care?

Whys Woven into Life

Why are there so many types of bread?
Do they have secret conventions?
Is sourdough feeling misled?
Or are they just baked with intentions?

Where does the music go at night?
Do stars hum lullabies to sleep?
Are they shy or just out of sight?
Creating dreams for us to keep?

Can a potato feel the heat?
Does it know it's going to fry?
Will it dance before it meets defeat?
Or just lie there, too shy to try?

Why do we always look for signs?
Do clouds write poetry up high?
Is every shadow hiding lines?
Or are we just asking to fly?

The Horizon of Uncertainty

Why does the sun never lose its way?
It rises and sets, then starts a new play.
What happens to clouds when they're feeling blue?
Do they drink up the rain, or just pass it to you?

If fish had feet, would they dance on the shore?
Would they twirl and leap, then ask for some more?
If cats wrote the rules, would naps be the law?
And would dogs then protest with a woof and a paw?

Pondering in Stillness

Do trees ever wonder where the squirrels go?
Or do they just listen to the rustling show?
If rocks could talk, what stories they'd scroll,
Of ancient escapades and a long-lost troll?

If I had a genie, what would I wish?
A lifetime of snacks? Or a pet goldfish?
Can a kite have dreams of flying so far,
That it ends up wedged in a tall, old car?

An Odyssey of the Mind

What makes the fridge hum in the dead of night?
Is it dreaming of cheese, or plotting a bite?
If socks had voices, would they sing a tune?
Or complain about washing machines that swoon?

Does the moon giggle when it plays hide and seek?
Does it wink at the stars while the night grows bleak?
If I asked a sandwich what it wants to be,
Would it answer, 'A star in the land of brie?'

Questions that Paint the Sky

Why do rainbows like to play peek-a-boo?
Do they hide in the clouds, sipping sky juice too?
If a butterfly lands with a wish on its wing,
Does it chant to the flowers or dance 'til they sing?

Do quokkas know they're the world's happiest fuss?
Or do they just chuckle and hop on a bus?
If clouds were made of cotton candy bright,
Would kids chase their dreams on a sugary flight?

Curiosity's Flame

Why can't cats speak to me, I wonder?
Do they plot while I sleep, like a thunder?
If I had wings, would I fly or just fall?
What if rubber ducks are really on call?

Are clouds just cotton candy in disguise?
Can I take a selfie of my own surprise?
Why does my dog bark at shadows so bright?
Is there a secret in the moonlight?

In Search of Answers

Why do socks vanish in the wash's spin?
Is there a sock monster hiding within?
How do we know if fish ever dream?
Can a taco truly reign supreme?

What makes a pizza extra cheesy?
Is it love, or just plain easy?
If I jump in puddles, will I float higher?
Does the sun smile when it gets a flyer?

Echoes of Inquiry

Do trees gossip when the wind whirls them near?
Do ants have caffeine when they scurry and cheer?
What do owls mean when they wisely hoot?
Is a snail just a slow-moving pursuit?

Why do we laugh when we're caught off guard?
Is humor the answer, or just a facade?
If I have two left feet, do I dance in style?
Can a question ever last a whole while?

Questions Beneath the Stars

Why do stars twinkle like a party's delight?
Can a comet confuse me with its flight?
What if clouds have feelings and feel blue?
Do they wish upon stars just like we do?

In the realm of night, do dreams take requests?
Can we tap dance with shadows, what a jest!
Are wishes born from bright moonbeams at play?
Or is it the universe just having its way?

The Ripple of Doubt

Why is the sky so high and blue?
Is it hiding all the answers too?
Questions float like ducks on a pond,
If I squint real hard, do they respond?

Why do socks seem to vanish in air?
Do they have secrets they no longer share?
Is the fridge a portal or just a door?
I check it for snacks, but find it a bore.

Can a sandwich really be made with care?
If I ask it nicely, will it repair?
Curiosity tickles like bees in my brain,
Maybe it's normal to go a bit insane.

What if the grass is actually green?
And the flowers just actors in an unseen scene?
The world spins questions like it's a game,
But who keeps the score? It's me, just the same.

Seeking Through Silence

In a world full of chatter, I pause and I think,
Are goldfish conspiring while I pour my drink?
Do trees gossip whispers amongst the leaves?
And if I ask nicely, will they share their grieves?

The elevator's silence feels thick as molasses,
Do awkward moments have secret classes?
Should I say 'hi' to the stranger near me?
Or point at the floor and flee like a bee?

If I squint at my cat, will she reveal truths?
What secret lives do her whiskers sooth?
Is she dreaming of quests in faraway lands?
Or just plotting my demise with her cunning plans?

Whispers in clutter of my dusty old brain,
Lead me to wonder if sanity's plain.
Because seeking through silence, it's clear and profound,
That the best question's always lost, never found.

Identity in Inquiry

Am I just a person who eats lots of pie?
Or the sum of my questions that flitter and fly?
Each query a puzzle, a piece of the whole,
That spins like confetti on a bright, sunny stroll.

Is my wallet just a store for receipts and regrets?
Or a treasure chest holding my best silly bets?
Do I wear my confusion like a scarf in the breeze?
Or is laughter a mirror, reflecting my ease?

Am I the sum of my socks, mismatched and bold?
Or a seeker of knowledge, with stories retold?
Tying questions like shoelaces, tight and real nice,
Maybe identity's better with a sprinkle of rice.

Each "why" and "how" is a step in the dance,
Inquiring for fun, oh, what a fine chance!
Let me collect my questions, they're mighty and spry,
In the circus of life, I'll be the clown who can fly.

Vistas of the Unknown

If I gaze at the stars, do they wink back at me?
Or are they just busy with cosmic TV?
What's cooking in space? A salad or stew?
Oh, the endless curiosities, like many a shoe.

Why does my cereal float when it's soaked?
Is it training for swimming, or merely a joke?
Do bananas co-host a show in the night?
Where they peel back their stories in comedic delight?

Is time a magician, pulling rabbits from hats?
Or a cat with nine lives, just teasing the bats?
Do we leap through existence like frogs on a log?
Or tiptoe through questions, avoiding the fog?

In the vistas of unknown, there's laughter to find,
Questions like butterflies, fluttering blind.
Embrace the absurd, let's leap and let fly,
For the laughter we harvest is what makes us high!

A Chorus of Whys

Why is the sky sometimes blue?
Why do my socks vanish too?
Why do cats sit on my books?
And why do I overlook all these nooks?

Where do the lost crumbs all go?
Who borrowed my favorite snow globe?
Why do trees dance in the breeze?
And do fish get cold in the freeze?

Why do we laugh till we cry?
What's so funny about a fly?
Why do we trip over our feet?
Are we meant to dance to the beat?

So many questions, what a delight!
Join in the fun, let's ponder tonight!
With laughter in mind, let's explore with glee,
The endless wonders of curiosity free!

The Inquisitive Tapestry

What's the secret of a good pie?
Why do bananas sometimes lie?
Is it wrong to wear shoes in bed?
And why do I keep losing my head?

Why does my goldfish do a twirl?
How does spaghetti make me swirl?
What if the sun just needs a rest?
Could the moon be shy, just like the rest?

Why does the dog dig around?
Who taught squirrels how to rebound?
Why do we sing in the shower?
And why does a flower have such power?

Each question leads to another silly thought,
In this tapestry of wonders, we've caught!
With laughter as our guiding light,
Let's keep asking, from day to night!

Mystery's Embrace

Why do we get lost in a maze?
What's so special about pizza days?
Why are shoes always mismatched?
And where has my lunch been dispatched?

How come the coffee's always cold?
What makes the toaster so bold?
Why does my cat think it's a king?
And why do we all love to sing?

Mysteries live in the heart of the fun,
Delighting us under the sun.
We chase questions, with a grin so wide,
In the sunny embrace, let's enjoy the ride!

So here's to the whys, let's have a blast!
The questions grow tall, but we'll never be last!
With laughter echoing through the air,
Join this playful mystery affair!

The Journey of Tomorrow's Questions

Where do socks go during the wash?
Is there a cat conspiracy, a secret nosh?
Why do we talk to ourselves at night?
And why does chocolate always feel right?

What if we could fly like a kite?
Can ducks ever take flight at night?
Why do we find such joy in a joke?
And is life just a whimsical hoax?

The road of questions never does slow,
With laughter and curiosity, we flow!
What's waiting at the end of our quest?
Could it be just more fun and jest?

So gather your whims, let's take a stroll,
On this vibrant journey, let's reach our goal!
With each giggle, we discover anew,
Life's funny secrets waiting for you!

The Dance of Doubt and Discovery

In the morning light, we wake up wide,
With questions swirling like a crazy ride.
Why is the sky blue, and what's the deal,
With socks that vanish? Do they have a wheel?

Curiosity twirls in a playful spin,
As we chase the answers, let the fun begin!
What's inside a taco? Is it pure bliss?
And why do we always forget our list?

Each little mystery a jig on the floor,
With laughter and smiles, we search for more.
Why do cats purr? Is it magic or fate?
Let's dance with our doubts, it's never too late!

So grab your questions and join in the fun,
In this wild waltz, we're never done.
Life's a silly game, so let's take a chance,
With laughter and queries, let's all do the dance!

Breathing Life into Queries

What if the earth giggles when we fall?
Do trees talk gossip, and do flowers call?
Is chocolate really just a fruit in disguise?
Or do gummy bears hold the secret to the skies?

With each breath we take, we ponder aloud,
Are fish saucy creatures, vastly proud?
Why do ducks quack in a waddle so neat?
And when do we decide that socks taste sweet?

Opening our minds creates a bright sky,
With whimsical thoughts that can soar and fly.
In the land of what-ifs, we stretch and bend,
Let's tickle the questions, not just pretend!

So take a deep breath, let curiosity flow,
As every question is a chance to grow.
From silly to serious, embrace the cheer,
In the dance of inquiry, let's shift into gear!

Shadows of Unanswered Thoughts

In the quiet of night, questions snicker and creep,
Are unicorns shy, or just lost in deep sleep?
Why do we wonder while under the moon?
Do socks commit crimes in the laundry cocoon?

With shadows that chuckle and sly little grins,
Do caterpillars think they'll dance when they spin?
What's on a donut's mind, round and sweet?
Do they squirm with delight when we eat?

Floating thoughts linger like fireflies in jars,
As we ponder the cosmos and think of the stars.
Why do we giggle at ghosts dressed in sheets?
Are they simply lost souls, or just craving sweets?

So dance with your shadows and laugh at the gloom,
For every odd question can brighten a room.
In the theater of thought, let's play and pretend,
With shadows of wonder, we'll never see end!

Navigating the Sea of Wonder

On a ship made of questions, we sail the vast seas,
With whales of imagination and swirling of breeze.
Why do seagulls squawk with such flair and loud?
Do they practice their solos to impress the crowd?

With each wave that crashes, a new thought will sprout,
Is the ocean just a big blue couch to lounge about?
Why does the sun set in a fiery show?
And where do the mermaids go when we don't know?

A treasure map drawn with ink from the sky,
Leads us to answers while we all laugh and fly.
Could frogs be the kings of a whimsical land?
Or do they just leap 'cause it's perfectly planned?

So raise up the sails, let's drift through the dreams,
In this journey of wonder, nothing is as it seems.
Life's a curious voyage, so come ride the tide,
With a boat full of questions, let's enjoy the ride!

Spheres of Understanding

In a world of endless chatter,
Why is my cat so fatter?
Do fish really dream of flight?
Or do they just swim, day and night?

I asked a frog about his throne,
He croaked back, 'Dude, I'm all alone!'
If trees could talk, what would they say?
'Just leaf me be, I hate this play!'

Illumination Through Inquiry

Why did the chicken cross the road?
To see if the grass was code?
But I've got questions, oh so many,
Like why is a penny worth a penny?

I asked my dog, 'What's life like?'
He wagged his tail, 'You mean the bike?'
Does the moon whimper when it's shy?
Or does it just wink and remind us why?

Reflections of an Inquirer

In the mirror, I ask my face,
'Why can't we all keep up the pace?'
If socks could talk, what would they wish?
'I'm tired of matching, it's quite a dish!'

I ponder things 'till skies grow dim,
Like why do we hum, when we begin?
Do clouds giggle when it rains?
Or do they just hide from silly pains?

Arrows of Curiosity

With arrows shot from questions bold,
I wonder if my coffee's cold?
What tales do the pillows weave at night?
Do they gossip about pillows in flight?

I'm on a quest, a qwerty spree,
Does the sun ever get bored of me?
Do whispers float like bubbles in air?
Or do they just hide from a cat's glare?

Searching for the Unseen

Why is the sky so blue, I ponder,
Is it paint, or simply a blunder?
Do clouds ever take a vacation,
Or are they stuck in their own formation?

Why do cats sit on laptops, so sly?
Are they plotting world domination, oh my!
Can socks go missing in the dryer's spin,
Or is there a portal to a sock-eating bin?

Is pizza a pie or a flat round treat?
Why do birds sing, do they have a beat?
If giraffes had neckties, would they look grand?
Or would they just look silly, don't you understand?

If fish could fly high, would they still swim?
What if pizza became a fruit, not a whim?
In this silly search, we laugh and play,
For questions keep boredom forever at bay!

Footprints in a Sea of Questions

Why do we park in driveways, I wonder?
And why is it called a hamburger, no thunder?
If we die in dreams, do we wake up puzzled?
Or do we just snore, a little muzzled?

Do cows ever say, 'Moo' in surprise?
Or do they just look at us with big, round eyes?
If light travels faster, how does it feel?
Is there a traffic jam on the way to the meal?

If I could talk to my goldfish today,
Would it tell me about its underwater ballet?
What if plants could dance, would they ask for a tune?
Or just sway back and forth, like under a moon?

In this sea of questions, I float with glee,
Each little thought, like bubbles flowing free.
For answers may come or may never align,
But the fun is in asking, and oh, how we shine!

Chasing Shadows of Truth

What's the sound of a shadow when it flees?
Does it whisper secrets carried by breeze?
If pencils have erasers, why don't they talk?
Would they doodle or giggle while taking a walk?

Do squirrels have meetings to plan their next heist?
And what do trees say when they're feeling nice?
If I ask my sandwich for wisdom today,
Would it giggle and simply crumble away?

Do rain clouds ever throw parties up high?
And do they invite the sun to stop by?
Why do we toast to things we can't see?
Is it for good luck or just for the tea?

In chasing these shadows, we dance without care,
For the questions we raise, float light in the air.
With humor our guide, we skip through the fun,
Searching for answers 'til our laughter is done!

Reflection on a Mystery

If mirrors could talk, what tales would they spin?
Would they gossip about who's really thin?
Do we reflect on thoughts we forgot to send?
Or just check if our hair has a funky bend?

What if our shoes were curious souls?
Would they ask why we step in puddles and holes?
If clocks could tick backwards, would time rewind?
Or would we just get dizzy, and lose our mind?

Why do we yawn when we're wide-awake?
Is it just our bodies playing a prank or mistake?
What if dogs could write, what stories would flow?
About chasing their tails, or barks in a show?

In the mirror of life where the questions arise,
We laugh at it all through our curious eyes.
For this mystery of living is funny and bright,
And the joy is in asking, day or night!

Riddles etched in Sand

Why did the chicken cross the street?
To find a joke that could compete.
But on the other side, it lost its way,
And now just wonders, 'What's for lunch today?'

Can fish really feel a splash of rain?
Or do they just swim without a brain?
In ocean's depths, they ponder and glide,
With bubble thoughts floating around inside.

Is a cat's curious stare a deep thought?
Or just a plan on how to steal that spot?
With paws on a throne, they reign supreme,
Yet still chase shadows, lost in their dream.

So here we sit, with questions galore,
While sand keeps slipping through the door.
Embrace the riddles; don't be bland,
For life is silly, like steps in sand.

The Beneath of What We Know

Why does the sun rise in the morn?
To wake up all the animals born.
But does it ever dread the light?
Maybe it dreams of a cozy night.

Are clouds just puffs of cotton candy?
Floating above, they look quite dandy.
And if it rains, do they feel sad?
Or just think, 'Damp fun isn't so bad?'

Do shadows have thoughts that they keep?
Or do they just follow, never to leap?
A dance in the dark, a hidden show,
What secrets lie in the places we go?

Beneath our knowing, laughs abound,
With giggles, chuckles, in questions found.
Let's ponder life with a playful poke,
In this grand question game we invoke.

Voices of Uncertainty

In a forest of doubts, we wander wide,
With squirrels debating their acorn pride.
Do trees ever listen to gossip above?
Or just sway along, in a breeze of love?

What do ducks quack about all day?
Are they critiquing how people play?
With waddle and wiggle, they seem so wise,
Chasing their tails, while we analyze.

If socks had voices, oh what would they say?
'Why do you lose us? We're here to stay!'
In the laundry's belly, they plot and scheme,
Spinning their tales in a fabric dream.

Here's to uncertainty; let's dance and twirl,
With giggles astir as our minds whirl.
In every question, a chuckle we find,
Voices of life, ever vibrant and kind.

Unmasking the Veil of Certainty

What's behind the curtain? Could it be fun?
A jester with riddles, or a needle and gun?
Peeking through layers of what we believe,
Where laughter and questioning dance and weave.

Do ants hold meetings to plan out their routes?
With tiny agendas, do they discuss doubts?
While we humans ponder, they march in a line,
In a world of certainty, they simply shine.

Is laughter just a way to bridge the gap?
Or a sneaky cover for another mishap?
With every giggle, a layer peels back,
Unmasking wisdom, in jokes that don't lack.

So let's lift the veil and join the jest,
Finding the joy in the questions we quest.
With humor as guide, we wander the earth,
In the grand game of life, what's your own worth?

Embracing the Unexplored

Why did the chicken cross the road?
To find what lay beyond the load.
With a wink and a cheeky grin,
It whispered, "Let the quest begin!"

A sock went lost without a trace,
It ventured out to find a place.
With every shoe it tried to find,
It laughed and danced, unconfined.

The cat on the roof began to prance,
In the moonlight, he took a chance.
"What if there's more than just this ledge?"
He leaped for joy, on a new edge!

So here we stand with silly thoughts,
Asking if we're simply dots.
The universe just shrugs and spins,
While we keep searching for the wins!

The Questions We Carry

Why do we park on driveways, pray tell?
And drive on the parkways, under the spell?
Each riddle wraps us tight and warm,
In a world where puzzling is the norm.

Is a hot dog a sandwich, so we muse,
Or a taco, or that thing we choose?
With every bite, it sparks delight,
Who knew food could fuel our night?

Do fish ever blush when they swim so sly?
Or snicker as they float on by?
We ponder deep, with grins so wide,
At the humor in this silly ride.

Questions float like bubbles in air,
Tickling brains with a cheeky flair.
With quirky quips and laughter too,
Who knew mysteries could be so blue?

Boundless Curiosities

What makes the grass so green and bright?
Does it envy clouds that take flight?
While worms wiggle in the earth below,
They giggle at what they do not know.

Why do we call them buildings when they're built?
Or swim in the sea yet feel no guilt?
With every glance and every glance,
The world does the silliest dance!

Do ducks really quack to share their thoughts?
Or simply gossip, tying up their knots?
We hop along with questions on deck,
In a parade of fun, what the heck?

With each new thought, we find a clue,
Bubbling laughter brews anew.
So grab your hat, let's hit the streets,
Curiosity leads to the silliest feats!

The Bonds of Wonderment

Why do we say 'it's a piece of cake'?
When baking makes so many quake?
In frosting dreams, we laugh and bake,
With every mix, we risk a shake!

What if our pets have secret chats?
Plotting tiny heists with their little hats?
As we ponder what they might say,
We giggle at their fluffy ballet.

Is a library just a quiet zoo,
Where books roam free, and ideas brew?
In whispers soft, they share their tales,
While chairs lean back and quietly wail.

Questions cling, like socks on a line,
Each one a twist in the grand design.
So let's grab joy, toss doubt aside,
And ride this wave of wonder with pride!

The Language of Inquiry

Why do ducks quack and run so fast?
Is it to flee from a bread crumb cast?
What's the secret behind a sneeze?
Does it make the universe sneeze?

Why are cats such a spark of flair?
Do they plot world domination from a chair?
Do they think that fish are just a snack?
And why do they always take a nap?

Why do old socks gather in a pile?
Could they be hatching a masterful style?
Will mushrooms ever start to dance?
Is this a dream or just happenstance?

Why can't I find my missing shoe?
Does it think it's funny, hiding from view?
Life's a puzzle without a clue,
So many questions, but where's the queue?

A Symphony of More Questions

If cows could moo in different tones,
Would they harmonize with wooden cones?
Can grapes ever dream of being wine?
Or is that just a silly sign?

Do spoons have a secret, cultish lore?
Do they envy forks for their rugged score?
Why do we fear spiders on the wall?
Should we just give them a fun call?

Is there a song for every shoe?
What would they sing, if they only knew?
Do toasters wish they could make a cake?
Or is it a secret that we can't shake?

What do jellybeans actually see?
Do they argue on who's the best, like me?
In the realm of questions, we roam free,
Twirling in laughter, come join the spree!

The Journey of Unasked Thoughts

What do clouds gossip about all day?
Do they laugh at sunbeams in a cheeky way?
Why do pages never seem to turn?
Is there a page-turning lesson to learn?

Do shadows have dreams in the dark?
Or do they just hang around to spark?
What if chairs could tell their tales?
Would they speak of people who always fail?

What would happen if grass could sing?
Would it compete with the bees in spring?
Do commas worry about their place?
And how would they feel in a racing race?

Why do pies have to cool on the sill?
Are they plotting to give a taste thrill?
Life's a journey that's full of jest,
Each question a clue, a curious quest!

In the Labyrinth of Whys

Why do ice cubes prefer a drink?
Is it for fun or to make us think?
Why is laughter contagious like glue?
Does it spread just to mess with you?

Is cereal better with milk or without?
Does the answer lead to a funny bout?
What if socks held a fashion show?
Would they strut down the floor, a real pro?

Can rainbows read our secret notes?
Or do they giggle while they float?
What does rice dream of while it cooks?
A best-selling novel or lovely books?

What's under a rock that's been in the sun?
Could it be secrets or just a pun?
As questions stack up in merry delight,
Let's giggle our way through the curious night!

Sifting Through the Ashes of Certainty

In a world made of cookies, I sit and munch,
Every crumb is a puzzle, a delightful lunch.
Why do spoons dress up as forks at night?
Perhaps they're just tired of a silver fight.

With a sparkler in hand, I check the stars,
Dodging the questions like speeding cars.
Is the moon really made of creamy cheese?
Or just a shiny pizza, designed to tease?

I ask my goldfish about life's big plans,
He just swims around with no visible hands.
Is that a wise fish, full of mystery?
Or just a swimmer trying to flee from me?

In a lab coat of dreams, I giggle and ponder,
What's with socks that vanish? I often wonder.
The answers float by like balloons in the sky,
But maybe it's fun just to ask and not try.

The Art of Preferring Mystery

Why do clowns juggle when they're feeling blue?
Maybe they think it's the easiest view.
Do unicorns ever play hide and seek,
Or just prance around, no hide-and-no-peek?

I wore mismatched shoes to dance in the rain,
Each step was a question, a sweet little bane.
Is that a puddle or a doorway to dreams?
All I know is it's bursting with giggly gleams.

With a wink, I flip pancakes sky high,
Do they ever wonder if they'll learn to fly?
Fluffy, round questions land on my plate,
Eggs crack open, oh what a fate!

I ride on a turtle, slow but steady,
In the race of life, I'm not quite ready.
But asking each question is quite the art,
Laughing with answers, that's how I start!

Stars that Blink in Question

Should I wear a hat made of tinfoil or lace?
Do aliens giggle in outer space?
The stars above wink, they dance in the night,
Is it just a game, or do they cast light?

A cat with a bowtie strolls by my door,
Is he on a mission, or just wanting more?
What if he's gathering secrets from trees,
And sharing with squirrels over cups of teas?

I peek through my window, waves of delight,
Is that the sun giving questions a fright?
Each ray is a riddle bouncing off glass,
Or just a spotlight for dogs that love to sass?

When I twirl in circles, my head feels quite spun,
Is chaos my partner, or am I the fun?
Together we leap through this perplexing quiz,
With laughter our guide, life's just one big whizz!

Seeking the Wisdom of Unspoken

In the land of misfit toys, I've found a clue,
Do they sit and ponder the same as we do?
When I ask my teddy bear, he shivers, then sighs,
Maybe he knows more than just cuddly ties.

A cactus named Fred passes me a note,
"Why don't we fashion this into a coat?"
Do needles dream of plump pillows at night,
Or are they just stuck in what feels just right?

Two dancing dandelions float by on the breeze,
Do they chat about wishes when they tease?
With each jaunty sway and laughter they share,
Could they truly know what we all must beware?

As I juggle balloons filled with giggles and grace,
I wonder which question will brighten my face.
In this game of life, where answers may hide,
It's the laughter of asking that makes it a ride.

The Scent of Intrigue

Why do cows wear bells, I ponder?
Is there a band I do not see?
Do llamas plot while I wander?
And what's up with my neighbor's tree?

Is cheese just a dream that once bloomed?
Or did it hide from me at the store?
Do socks have feelings when they're doomed?
Ah, the questions I can't ignore!

Dialogues with the Universe

Hey moon, what's your dream at night?
Do stars gossip? Spill the tea?
Do planets feel lonely in flight?
And where do all lost socks flee?

Living on a spinning ball, how strange!
Do ants have meetings about our feet?
Do clouds ever think, 'Time for a change?'
Or is rain just their way to cheat?

Paths Woven from Wonder

If a tree falls, does it make a sound?
And what if the squirrel's on a quest?
Does grass feel tickled when I'm around?
Oh, to be the crow, just feel blessed!

Do shadows debate how to act?
Are plants secretly judging my style?
What if my cat wrote a book, in fact?
A memoir that's truly worthwhile!

Into the Depths of Inquiry

Why does the toaster get so hot?
Is it mad about its breadly fate?
Do goldfish dream of swimming spots?
And can bananas contemplate?

Does the fridge hum a soothing tune?
Are spoons secretly longing to race?
Why does coffee shout in the afternoon?
And why can't I find my place?

In Search of Wonder

Why do we giggle at rubber ducks?
Is it the quack or the silly luck?
Do socks go missing for a copper dime?
Or do they plot to drape in mystic rhyme?

What's the secret of the jellybeans?
Are they hiding in candy-coated scenes?
If I might ask, will pets start to dance?
And make their owners join in the prance?

Why do pigeons coo like they own the place?
Claiming all streets with such bold grace?
If leaves could laugh, what would they say?
Would they tease the wind in a playful way?

So here I roam, with questions galore,
Searching for wonders that burst from the core,
With chuckles and queries as friends in tow,
Life's a big joke, come join the show!

Questions Beneath the Stars

Do stars get tired of twinkling bright?
Do they wish upon themselves every night?
Are moonbeams ticklish, laughing in space?
Or simply smiling at the human race?

When clouds bump into each other, do they hug?
Or just complain about the weather's tug?
If I asked a comet, would it go zoom?
And leave behind a trail of cosmic bloom?

Why do cats sit like they know all the things?
Possessing wisdom that makes our hearts sing?
Can fish in the sea ever purr in delight?
Or are they just splashing in pure moonlight?

And what is it like to have a goldfish grand?
Do they chat about bubbles, as we've all planned?
Under this sky, with questions to unfurl,
There's laughter in asking, it's quite the whirl!

Whispers of Inquiry

If my dog could speak, what tales would spill?
About squirrels that challenge his daily thrill?
Do they plot his downfall or just play a game?
With barks and whines, do they share the same fame?

Why do bicycles get so jealous of shoes?
Is it the arches or all the cruising views?
If flowers could giggle, would they bud into cheer?
Counting the raindrops that fall every year?

How come ice cream melts before I can eat?
Is it a plot or just summer's sweet heat?
Why do we call it a 'coughing fit'?
Does it ever stop to think it's a hit?

In this curious world where questions abound,
I'll roam with whimsy, let laughter resound,
With each silly query, the moments will blend,
In a symphony playful that never must end!

Unraveling Curiosity's Thread

What if spaghetti could wiggle and dance?
And meatballs were kings in a saucy romance?
Do pancakes dream of heights like the sky?
While butter's just waiting for the perfect pie?

If toasters could talk, would they share all their burns?
Or maybe just gossip about pastry turns?
What secrets do leaves whisper while we sleep?
In the rustling wind, are promises to keep?

Do shadows have fun while they're chasing the light?
Or make up tall tales on a starry night?
Are rainstorms just children in playful disguise?
Splashing around with mischievous sighs?

In this world filled with quirks and oddity flair,
Every quirky question hangs sweet in the air,
With laughter, we wander, with wonder we tread,
In a quest for the silly, with joy, we are led!

Questions that Shape the Soul

Why is the sky such a lovely hue?
Can fish really swim, or are they just blue?
Do clouds have a job, floating up high?
Or do they just loaf, and eat apple pie?

What's the deal with socks, always in pairs?
Do they conspire while hiding from stares?
If a tree falls alone, does it still make a sound?
Infinite questions swirl all around!

If cats have nine lives, what's their grand goal?
Is it just to nap? Oh, how they control!
Do ants have a plan, marching as one?
Or are they just lost, looking for fun?

Does the sun throw parties when day turns to night?
Or is the moon the DJ, grooving with light?
What makes a sandwich the best on the shelf?
Is it really about us, or just about itself?

The Quest for Understanding

If life's a riddle, what's the punchline?
Is it hidden in laughs, or locked in a shrine?
Do rainbows have secrets, or just pretty ends?
And why do my leftovers always have friends?

Why do we drive on parkways, then park on the street?
Do ducks wear their quacks like fancy elite?
Do rocks feel the weight of the world on their back?
Or are they just chillin' on an eternal track?

Is cheese the answer, all crumbly and bold?
Does it make our dreams tastier, or is that just old?
When seeds have a meeting, what do they discuss?
Maybe the best way to be sprouted with fuss?

Is laughter a code that we all can decode?
Or just gibberish told on a bumpy old road?
How many licks does it take to get clear?
And does the owl wonder if it's night all year?

Shimmering Threads of Wonder

If popcorn likes movies, where does it go?
Is there a theater for snacks, in the know?
Do turtles ever ponder the speed of their race?
Or chill in their shells, with a smile on their face?

When does a trampoline start feeling springy?
Do jellybeans giggle, or just feel zingy?
If clouds play hide and seek, who's it that wins?
Is it the sun that just laughs, while it spins?

Why do we call it a 'freezer' in spite?
Is it really so generous, giving us ice?
If socks were to vote, would they pick a pair?
Or do they just wish they could float in the air?

Are marshmallows happy when turned into fluff?
Or do they get sad, feeling not good enough?
What makes a pancake the best of the bunch?
Is it the syrup, or just a good crunch?

Inquiries of the Heart

If love is a puzzle, where's the big piece?
Could laughter be glue and help us find peace?
When does a hug turn into a dance?
And why do we smile at the silliest chance?

Can joy be wrapped up, like a gift in a box?
Or is it found under mismatched socks?
Do dreams have a playlist, all set to ignite?
Or do they just pop up in the middle of night?

Why do we fumble with words that we say?
Is it just part of our quirky display?
When do stars giggle, twinkling like mad?
Or do they just wish on wishes we've had?

If hearts can ask questions, what would they find?
Are we just up here, totally unrefined?
What makes a friendship the best we can share?
Is it the fun, or just knowing we care?

Echoes in the Silence

In the quiet, I wander, every thought a balloon,
Searching for answers, with a silly tune.
Why are socks always missing, in the laundry's embrace?
Maybe they dodge questions, seeking a new place.

Clouds pass overhead, with riddles they share,
What do they whisper, floating up there?
Do they laugh at my queries, tossed in the air?
Or just fluffing their pillows without any care?

A cat on the windowsill pretends to be wise,
Is it plotting world domination or just chasing flies?
Every blink is a secret, hidden from sight,
What's under its fur? I'm tempted to bite!

So I sit with a sandwich, pondering the day,
Wondering why butter always spills in dismay.
With giggles and guffaws, questions dance in my mind,
In the echo of silence, answers stay blind.

The Quest for Unfathomable Truths

With a magnifying glass, I roam through the park,
Why do ducks quack loudly when it gets dark?
Do they hold secret meetings to discuss their fate?
Or are they just hungry for a snack on a plate?

I asked a wise owl, perched high on a tree,
Why do you hoot? What's your mystery?
He blinked with a feathered shrug, looked at me funny,
Maybe he thought my questions weren't worth any honey.

Between bites of cheese, I ponder the night,
Do stars feel lonely, or is it just bright?
What if they giggle, lighting up the skies,
Having their fun while we ponder and sigh?

So here's to the questions, profound and absurd,
To the whispers of answers, sometimes unheard.
In this silly adventure, what truths will I find?
Just a bunch of giggles, or maybe a rhyme.

Between the Lines of Existence

In a world full of scribbles, I seek to unwind,
Why do most pancakes flip, but some stay aligned?
Is there a council that judges their fate?
Or do they just choose to lounge on the plate?

I asked a goldfish what secrets it hides,
Why it swims in circles, as if it decides.
With a blink and a bubble, it looks so profound,
Maybe it knows things I still haven't found.

With crayons and chaos, I scribble my dreams,
Do clouds plot their stories, with whimsical schemes?
What if they play chess, those fluffy white kings,
Staying just out of reach while the world spins and swings?

As laughter dances lightly through giggles and grins,
I chase after answers, like a kid at chins.
In shadows and sunlight, I'm lost in the quest,
Finding joy in the journey, it's truly the best.

Why the Sky Holds Its Breath

Look high in the sky, it's a riddle in blue,
Why does it blush pink when the sun bids adieu?
Does it play hide and seek, with the stars all aglow,
Or is it saving up whispers for the moon's soft show?

I wondered aloud, as the breeze tangled my hair,
Can clouds feel ticklish, floating without a care?
What if they chuckle, as we all gaze in awe,
At the ballet of shadows and the light of the stars?

With a donut in hand, I ponder and muse,
Does the universe giggle, or does it just snooze?
Every blink of a star could be calling my bluff,
Maybe to remind me that pondering's tough!

So let's keep asking in a world full of fun,
With each silly question, another's begun.
In laughter and curiosity, we flee from the dread,
'Cause who knows the answers? Maybe donuts instead!

Inquisitive Hearts

Why is the sky so blue and bright?
Do fish ever get tired of the light?
If I wear socks with my sandals, will I be a fashion hit?
Or simply blend in with the people who don't give a wit?

Why do cats choose to knock things down?
Is it their mission to make us frown?
If I learn to cook, will I be a chef?
Or merely create dishes that are better left bereft?

Do we really need to nap at noon?
Or can we just dance with a mop and a broom?
If I question and seek, what will I find?
Maybe just answers that tickle my mind.

What's the secret of the universe, pray?
A joke that the cosmos forgot to say?
With questions galore, I laugh and I ponder,
In this world of wonder, my mind will wander.

Wandering Minds

What's the deal with socks that disappear?
Did they form a union and migrate, I fear?
Do fridge magnets gossip while we're away?
Or do they just collect dust on a rainy day?

When did cheese become such a big deal?
Does it sing when it's melting? Do you think it can feel?
Why do we park on driveways, but drive on the street?
Is this the start of a riddle or just a repeat?

If cheese had a hat, what would it be?
A top hat for cheddar? What else could we see?
Do dogs think we're silly for talking to them?
Or do they just plot world dominance, on a whim?

Why does the toaster only burn my bread?
Is it mad because I haven't petted its head?
With thoughts that bounce like an overcooked ball,
I'll keep asking questions, both big and small.

Beneath the Surface of Certainty

Is there really a hidden camera show?
Where all of our quirks put on quite the show?
Do clouds float by, thinking, 'What's next to see?'
Or are they pondering life's great mystery?

Do we age like fine cheese or get stinky with time?
If I could rewind, would there be a crime?
Why do ducks quack with such confidence bold?
Are they just pranksters, or wise tales retold?

What if rainbows are just color spills?
Left from the laughter of whimsical hills?
Is jelly the secret code of the universe?
Or just a condiment dressed up in a verse?

Underneath the certainty, doubt finds a way,
Inviting more questions to brighten the day.
With laughter and quirks, let's ponder the whole,
In the comedy of life, let's play our role.

The Why Behind the What

What's the reason behind our morning brew?
Is it magic beans, or just something new?
Do clocks laugh at us when we snooze away?
Or just keep ticking, come what may?

Why do we insist that cats own the house?
Is it because they think we're just a big mouse?
If I talk to my plants, do they understand?
Or do they just dream of a tropical land?

What makes us tick, what makes us dance?
Is it chocolate or simply a chance?
Why does pizza taste better at night?
Is it the moonlight or toppings just right?

With each silly question, I giggle and grin,
Finding joy in the chaos that life has spun.
In this dance of wonder, we flirt with the odd,
Laughing at questions like a cheerful façade.

The Dance of Doubts

Why do we worry about what will become?
Is it the popcorn that's making us numb?
Do cookies hold secrets in their crispy layers?
Or are they just sweets with no other players?

What does a goldfish think when it swims all day?
Just circling around, or lost in its play?
If life is a dance, am I stepping right?
Or tripping over shoes, singing out of sight?

Are unicorns just horses with marketing dreams?
Or is there magic dust in the sunlight they beam?
Why do we giggle at things that are strange?
Is it the humor in life's endless range?

In each dance of doubt, laughter unfolds,
As we twirl with our questions, both timid and bold.
So let's jiggle through life, embrace the unknown,
In this playful adventure, we're never alone.

When Questions Paint the Horizon

Why did the chicken cross the road?
To find out where all the light bulbs glowed.
The cow jumped over the moon last night,
Searching for answers in the starry flight.

Bouncing ideas like a rubber ball,
Does it matter if the cat's big or small?
The dog just cocks his head and grins,
Is pondering life where the real fun begins?

Little kids with their endless 'why',
Turn the world into a puzzling sky.
Silly things make the best of us laugh,
Like asking a fish about its next path.

In the circus of thoughts that turn and swirl,
Life's a waltz in a questioning whirl.
Grab that clown nose, what's next on the list?
Is the secret found, or just the gist?

The Heartbeat of Wondering

What's fluffier, a cloud or a sock?
Do fish really know how to shock?
Why do shoes always lose their mate?
Is every puzzle just a twist of fate?

Tickle a thought and watch it dance,
Wonder if life is just happenstance?
The cat in the hat knows where to go,
But where's that whiskered fellow to show?

With marshmallows bouncing in hot cocoa,
I ask, is that the best way to throw?
Peanut butter and jelly, a classic pairing,
But who decided it was worth sharing?

While juggling humor with a dash of rue,
What questions linger beneath skies so blue?
In laughter, we find those shining threads,
Life's riddle tied with whimsical leads.

Musings on the Edge of Belief

Is the moon made of cheese, I ask with cheer?
Or is it just dairy, floating near?
Aliens laughing in their green space car,
Plotting a prank from a million miles far.

Penguins skate in tuxedos on ice,
Do they wonder too about life's slice?
While socks run away as if on a quest,
Do they dare ask who's wearing the best?

Why are there bubbles in fizzy drinks?
Do they giggle as they form and clink?
Chasing the thoughts that swirl in my head,
What if we woke up and weren't even bred?

So crack open a book and bite on a pen,
Questions dance like wild mice in a den.
In the mirth of inquiry, we take a dip,
Life's an adventure on a cosmic trip!

Beneath the Surface of Knowing

Do clouds ever weigh their fluffy plight?
And what about ants, can they take flight?
If a tree falls, does it make a sound?
What if it happens where no one's around?

Each riddle's a door to a feathery dream,
Like fish that dance in a bubble-filled stream.
Why do we giggle when things go awry?
Maybe laughter's just a wink from the sky.

Why do we ask but rarely receive?
Is searching for answers a way to believe?
Do owls hoot to spark a great chat,
Or is it just because they're good at that?

Amidst the banter of thoughts that twirl,
Questions pop like popcorn in a whirl.
So let's lift our eyebrows, give a good cheer,
For the joy of wondering is the best souvenir!

www.ingramcontent.com/pod-product-compliance
Lightning Source LLC
Chambersburg PA
CBHW051653160426
43209CB00004B/887